My Little Golden Book About
San Francisco

By Toyo Tyler

Illustrated by Courtney Dawson

🐾 A GOLDEN BOOK • NEW YORK

Library of Congress Control Number: 2020934952
ISBN 978-0-593-30118-0 (trade) — ISBN 978-0-593-30119-7 (ebook)
Printed in the United States of America
10 9 8 7 6 5 4 3 2

Hello! My name is Sally the Sea Lion, and this is my home—**San Francisco**, the City by the Bay, located in northern California. I'm off to visit my friends at Seal Rock, across the city. Would you like to come with me? We'll take the scenic route!

When I'm not lounging on one of the docks at **Pier 39**, I sometimes take a ride on the carousel, explore the shops, and even get my portrait drawn. How do I look?

Just a few piers away is the heart of **Fisherman's Wharf**. People from all over the world come here for the delicious seafood. *Mmmmm!* Do you smell that? Sourdough bread bowls with clam chowder—my favorite!

In the middle of San Francisco Bay is **Alcatraz Island**. You can take a ferry there (if you don't have flippers like I do) and tour the abandoned prison.

Our next stop is **Ghirardelli Square**, which used to be a chocolate factory. Even though the factory closed many years ago, there is still an ice cream and chocolate shop. Let's go in for a treat!

Everything looks delicious! What shall we get?

A chocolate-covered strawberry . . .

a sea-salt caramel chocolate bar . . .

or an ice cream sundae
with hot fudge, bananas,
and whipped cream?
(Hmm, I wonder if they can
add sardine sprinkles to that!)

Hop aboard and hold on tight!

O'FARRELL & HYDE

42
CABLE CAR

This **cable car** will take us
up, up, UP . . .

and down, down, DOWN the hills
of San Francisco! Ding, ding, ding!
Watch out, everyone—
here we come!

Let's explore **Chinatown**! This neighborhood is full of bright red lanterns, green-tiled roofs, delicious steamed buns, and busy markets. You may even spot a dragon!

A short walk from Chinatown is **Little Italy**. Waddle down Columbus Avenue with me and smell all the pizza. From here you can see the **Transamerica Pyramid**—one of the tallest buildings in the city!

One of San Francisco's most famous landmarks is the **Ferry Building**. The 245-foot-tall clock tower greets travelers who arrive in the city by ferryboat.

Inside the Ferry Building is a marketplace filled with fruits, teas, honeys, olive oils, cheeses, baguettes . . . and even scrumptious lobster potpies!

Head to the ferry terminal for the best view of the **Bay Bridge**. This double-decker bridge connects San Francisco to Oakland. It is one of the longest suspension bridges in the United States!

Say hello to some of my feathered friends on **Telegraph Hill**! These pretty birds are wild cherry-headed conure parrots.

Keep climbing the steps to the very top of the hill and you'll reach **Coit Tower**, known for its beautiful murals and breathtaking views of the city and the bay.

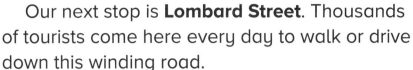

Our next stop is **Lombard Street**. Thousands of tourists come here every day to walk or drive down this winding road.

Pssssst! Want to hear a secret? Even though Lombard Street is known as the crookedest street in the world, there's an even *more* crooked street in San Francisco— Vermont Street!

Let's take a stroll along the waterfront to see the world-famous **Golden Gate Bridge**. It's the tallest bridge in the United States, and there are three ways to cross it: walk, drive, or bike!

To go from one "golden" landmark to another, our next destination is **Golden Gate Park**. There are so many things to do here! We can . . .

visit the albino alligator at the **California Academy of Sciences** . . .

take a pedal boat around **Stow Lake** . . .

sip green tea at the
Japanese Tea Garden . . .

and stop to smell the roses
at the **Rose Garden**.

On the western edge of San Francisco, you'll find three miles of sand and surf. Welcome to **Ocean Beach**! The water is too rough for swimming, but you can enjoy a picnic, build a sandcastle, fly a kite, or look for little white shorebirds called snowy plovers.

Behind me is **Cliff House**—
a restaurant that has been a
part of San Francisco for more
than 150 years!

We made it to **Seal Rock**! Thank you for joining me on my journey across one of the most spectacular cities in the world. San Francisco definitely gets my *seal* of approval!